Introduction

Ludlow sits on a ridge above the Rive
certainly occupied by prehistoric tribes.
essentially Norman and its compact me
the castle, first built by the de Lacy family, has l   , saved
from unwanted 20thC development. There are tw   ...ing from the
medieval period: the church of St Laurence and   .v Castle, which are
major landmarks which can be seen for miles around; you will enjoy many
superb views from the walks in this book.

The town has charmed many travel writers through the decades, including
John Betjeman, who was most complimentary. It is not only the medieval
street pattern that is so engaging, but also the elegant Georgian houses that
have survived. Broad Street is possibly one of finest streets in the country.
Needless to say, the onslaught of traffic and the chain stores which seek to
dominate small towns has begun to change its character; the challenge will be
to respect what we have whilst offering a warm welcome to visitors.

Ludlow is also known as one of the major centres in the country for 'slow
food' and the local group seeks to support smaller sustainable food producers
in the area, many of which can be found at the twice monthly Local Produce
Market in the Market Square. There are other places which stand out, such as
Glebe Farm Tearooms at Hopesay and the Green Café in Ludlow. The authors
of this book seek to promote 'Slow Travel' in the Marches by encouraging
people to immerse themselves in the locality and this book fits this approach
well. Ludlow is currently seeking to become a 'Walkers Welcome' town.

Mortimer Country lies to the west and south west of Ludlow towards
the Radnorshire hills of Wales, just a short ride by bus, train or bicycle. It
is a deeply rural enclave with a richness and diversity of landscapes from
rolling wooded hills to revered riverside meadows. The Arrow, Clun, Lugg
and Teme rivers are all designated as Sites of Special Scientific Interest.
There are numerous castles, churches and historic houses open to the public,
plus villages with rural inns of character. There are also a small number of
attractions such as the Aardvark Bookery at Brampton Bryan and Croft Castle,
near Yarpole, which are ideal places for the walker to visit.

Ludlow is well served by train from Cardiff and Manchester. It also has a
network of buses, including some out to the villages, most of which are two
hourly. On summer Sundays and Bank Holidays the Castle Connect service
runs through Mortimer Country. If you are unsure about a bus or train time
it is best to contact 'traveline' on 0171 200 2233 for buses and 'National Rail
Enquiries – 08457 484950 for train times. There's also a good website:
www.travelshropshire.co.uk which contains much local transport information, including current bus timetables.

Enjoy your walks!

CORVE CIRCULAR

DESCRIPTION An unusual 8 mile walk that starts at Ludlow station (special attraction The Ludlow Brewing Company brewery tap, open daily except Sundays), heads out of town along the River Corve across flat fields to the pretty hamlet of Stanton Lacy. Leaving the Corve the route climbs gently at first on a road, then steeply up the side of The Hope to a fine viewing point before returning back to the river plain and Ludlow. There are many cafes and pubs which offer refreshment in Ludlow including Good Beer Guide entries the Church Inn and the Queens.

START & FINISH Ludlow Railway Station SO 512751.

DIRECTIONS The walk starts at Ludlow station, easily reached by train or bus; parking available at Galdeford Car Park nearby.

I From the station walk towards the supermarkets and then at the traffic lights, go RIGHT into Corve Street. After 250 yards take the RIGHT fork into Lower Corve Street past the Unicorn pub. At the end, cross over then turn RIGHT heading under the railway bridge. At the mini roundabout go LEFT onto Fishmore Road. Walk along here until you go over the A49. Shortly after the bridge take the track LEFT signposted to Elm Lodge.

2 Follow the footpath signs which keep you to the right alongside a hedge and fence. At the gate and cattle grid the footpath is on the left of the driveway to the house called Redhill. The path is well signed and crosses two stiles then turns right to follow the field edge through two fields via two kissing gates to go through a gate at the top of the hill. The path carries straight on but is now following the left hand edge of two fields with fine views towards Clee Hill on your right. At the bottom of the second field the path turns LEFT over two stiles and then passes along the bottom of a large field with a stream on your right.

3 Pass through the kissing gate and join a track down the River Corve that takes you towards a farm and to a bridge over the river. Just after the bridge go RIGHT through the walkers' gate to follow the edge of the field alongside the river now heading upstream. There is a gate at the end of the first field and then you continue, following the river bank through a second field to a gate. *There are a number of alders along this bank that attract a good number of siskins in winter and early spring.*

4 When you join the track at the edge of the golf course/racecourse, go RIGHT and follow for about 300 yards. Before the B road go RIGHT through a parking area to a way-marked path that leads over a stile into a field. Cross the stile and head toward the gap in the trees straight in front of you. This takes you to the edge of the Corve and now follow this until you reach a large footbridge over the river. Go RIGHT over the bridge then LEFT continuing to follow the river bank upstream. Walk ahead, crossing two stiles through two fields until a final stile leads onto a track past some houses. Now join the road in front of St Peter's Church in Stanton Lacy, thought to have Saxon origins. *In medieval times, the village was associated with the de Lacy family who built and settled into Ludlow Castle. In spring this ancient churchyard is famously full of snowdrops and is well worth a visit.*

5 Turn RIGHT on the road and then at the T-junction LEFT. Follow this minor road for ½ mile until it meets a larger road. Cross straight over here and go through the right-hand gate. This track, which can be overgrown, leads to a large field the centre of which you cross heading steeply upwards looking for the gate on the far side which is just to the right of the telegraph pole. Go through the gate and continue climbing in a newly-planted wood and through the gate at the top. *Look behind you for views of the racecourse and beyond that to Bringewood.* Cross the field walking towards the barn then through a gate.

6 Turn RIGHT crossing the cattle grid and walk along the metalled track. This is the high point of this walk so take time to enjoy the views. After a while the track heads downhill and becomes quite steep just before it joins a minor road. Turn LEFT and after about 30 yards look for a stile RIGHT into the field. Cross straight over the field and through the metal field gate. Keep RIGHT here and follow the stream down. By the field corner bear LEFT by the hedge and cross the stile RIGHT, then head half LEFT down to a double field gate. There is a pedestrian gate to the right of this which takes you onto the road. Turn LEFT on the road and walk along here past the first house and then just before the second house (called Whitbatch Cottage) go RIGHT over a stile into the field. Keep the hedge dividing the two fields on your right. Walk to the far end of the field and then turn LEFT. After a short distance you will cross a stream and then turn immediately LEFT, rejoining the path you came out on.

7 Retrace your steps crossing the double stile and then with the hedge on your right side to the top of the hill – again with good views of Clee Hill. Cross the stile into the field and with the hedge on your left walk past the house and continue down until you come to the stile on your left. The path now turns right and brings you out at a stile on the metalled track past the house and barn on your right and then joins the track from Elm Lodge. At the road turn RIGHT back over the A49, along Fishmore Road, RIGHT at the mini-roundabout, LEFT once you have passed underneath the railway bridge and so back to the traffic lights where a LEFT turn takes you back to the station.

3

WALK 2
LUDLOW TO CAYNHAM

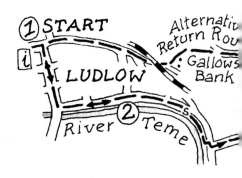

DESCRIPTION This 7½ mile walk (4 miles if you decide to start at the Eco Park) offers a mix of town walks, country lanes and field paths leading to Caynham Iron Age hillfort and Caynham parish church then back by Ledwyche, both names being of Saxon origin. There are some exceptional views of Clee Hill, and Mortimer Forest as well as the Malvern Hills in the distance.

START & FINISH Ludlow Market Square, Visitor Information Centre/Assembly Rooms SO 510746.

DIRECTIONS Ludlow is easily reached by bus or train, and the Market Square is the town's meeting point. This walk starts by the Visitor Information Centre at the Assembly Rooms where some buses stop, including the town service that runs to the Eco Park if you wish to shorten the walk. There is a car park nearby or at the Eco Park

I With your back to the Visitor Information Centre turn RIGHT along High Street to the Buttercross. Turn RIGHT to walk down one of the loveliest streets in England, under the last remaining Ludlow gateway to the traffic lights by the Ludford Bridge. Cross here and turn LEFT to walk by the River Teme and ahead into Temeside. The path narrows on the right so cross over and continue ahead along the pavement.

2 As the road bends left go RIGHT at the junction by an old toll house and continue along Temeside until the road begins to curve left. Cross over, climb a stile on the right, follow a delightful path LEFT alongside the Teme. It soon cuts LEFT to climb steps to a road. Go RIGHT and then LEFT at the junction into Foldgate Lane. Follow this, ignoring the next junction right to Foldgate Farm. It is narrow with a sharp left hand bend so beware of traffic. When the lane bends to a mini-roundabout continue ahead to the Sheet Road. Turn RIGHT to cross the road and walk ahead to the A49 road (super-

market to the right). Go over the pelican crossing then follow the path ahead to the turning for the Eco Park but keep ahead. For those joining here at the Eco Park (bus stop on the left) go back to the Sheet Road, cross over and TURN LEFT.

3 Continue ahead through Sheet and then onward along the road (no pavement) into countryside. If you decide to face the traffic make sure you cross back over before the road bends right. Look for a stile on the left. Cross it and head slightly RIGHT down the field on the Shropshire Way to a gated footbridge across the Ledwyche Brook. Now, climb up the field in a similar direction to cross a stile near a large oak tree. Once over, head slightly LEFT again to cross a stile by a gate. Go slightly RIGHT to join a green track and onward through scrub to a stile. Climb over into woodland. The path runs ahead at first then curves RIGHT and rises sharply up the embankment to a stile. Cross this to enter the enclave of Caynham Camp. *This large Iron Age hillfort was built in three stages and several 'digs' have uncovered the lifestyle of these early settlers who inhabited the camp from 800 BC through to 100 BC.*

4 Head slightly LEFT to walk between the earthworks. This includes walking through the eastern entrance of the fort between the ramparts. Cross a stile by a barred gate and go slightly RIGHT to cross another into a field. Keep ahead in a similar direction to cross two stiles in two boundaries. You reach a gate and stile; do not cross but instead turn RIGHT to follow hedge now on your left. Just before the corner, go

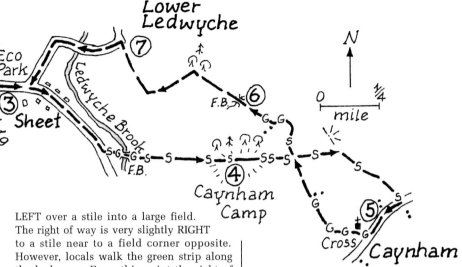

Lower
Ledwyche

Caynham
Camp

Cross
Caynham

LEFT over a stile into a large field. The right of way is very slightly RIGHT to a stile near to a field corner opposite. However, locals walk the green strip along the hedgerow. From this point the right of way is directly ahead with your back to the stile, aiming for an electricity pole. At that point the map shows the path cutting LEFT to pass by two remnant oak trees and onwards to a stile in the hedge ahead. Once again, locals simply continue along the green strip alongside the field. Cross the stile LEFT onto the road and go RIGHT to a lay-by.

5 Turn RIGHT through a gate into the churchyard to pass by the 14thC preaching cross. *The pretty church was extensively re-built in the 19thC.* Continue to the entrance of St Mary's church. Then at the western end go slightly RIGHT to exit at a gate. Keep ahead on a path, slightly right, across the field to a gate. Once through turn RIGHT to walk along an old tree lined track up to a barred gate. Go through it and keep LEFT with the hedge on your left, climbing to pass a stile on your left (crossed earlier) and to a stile ahead. Cross this and keep ahead along the hedge to a waymark post. Go RIGHT by the corrugated iron shelter and by an isolated stile to your left. Your way is ahead on a green track by bushes and then curving LEFT down to a gate and woodland. Continue ahead and go through a second gate into a field. Head across the field in the same direction towards a gateway, but just before, cut RIGHT down to a footbridge.

6 Continue ahead on a green track across the field, rising towards a wood. The track runs alongside it and bends slightly LEFT to descend to a point where it bends RIGHT and runs ahead to a junction. Go LEFT here through a gap by a gate into Lower Ledwyche. Turn LEFT onto Squirrel Lane and follow this until it joins the Sheet Road.

7 Cross over and go RIGHT to retrace your steps back to the Eco Park (return bus stop is on the right) or onward to walk back into town, across the A49 to the junction by the supermarket. Cross the pelican crossing (ahead) and turn LEFT then RIGHT into Parys Road. Cross over and keep ahead at first but go LEFT on the bridleway signposted to Sandpits. As this rises and bends right, go ahead over a stile onto a green common known as Gallows Bank. Descend to the bottom to enter a short road. Walk ahead and LEFT onto Sidney Road, then RIGHT along the path signposted as an 'alternative route' which cuts LEFT under the railway. Turn RIGHT on the pavement along Sheet Road and Galdeford to the Queens public house (a good place for refreshment!) then ahead along Tower Street to the Bull Ring. Cross the main road and walk ahead along King Street to your start point.

PRIORS HALTON CIRCULAR

DESCRIPTION A fine circular 5½ mile wander from Ludlow Market Square that follows the Mortimer Trail up to Mary Knoll then drops steeply then to climb through the 'secret' Mary Knoll valley before dropping through open countryside with great views back towards the town. This offers a superb contrast between woodland and open countryside in South Shropshire. Mortimer Forest is managed by the Forestry Commission and there are number of waymarked circular routes including a Geology Trail. There are refreshments at the Green Café or in town.

START & FINISH Ludlow Market Square, Visitor Information Centre SO 510746.

DIRECTIONS Ludlow is easily reached by bus or train, and the Market Square with castle gates is the town's meeting point. There is a car park behind the Market Square. The route heads down behind the castle to the River Teme that loops round the town.

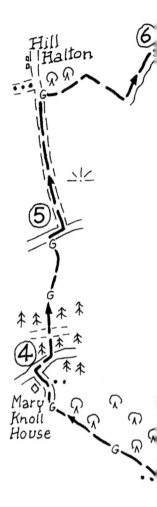

I With your back to the Visitor Information Centre go LEFT towards Ludlow Castle. Take Dinham, the road to the left of the Castle or the footpath to the right and drop down to the Millennium Green at the edge of the River Teme. Cross Dinham bridge and then head up the steps that are straight in front of you into the woods. Keep to the right edge of the woods and when you meet the road turn RIGHT. At the junction on the hair pin bend go LEFT and after 100 yards there is a clearly marked track to the LEFT. Follow this rising steadily, keeping to the right at the fork until the path curves sharp left and the road is reached by a small car parking area.

2 Cross the road and head into Mortimer Forest on a broad stony track passing the Forestry Commission offices. Continue on this track as it rises – *there are good views looking back towards Clee Hill.* After a while you will pass a seat on your right, after which take the next path off RIGHT and follow it

through to a seat – *where there are superb views towards High Vinnals and further in the distance into Wales.*

3 From the seat return to the broad track and start descending RIGHT. Join the larger forestry road but look out for a path RIGHT – signed Climbing Jack Path. This footpath descends very steeply. *The exposed stone banks have an alpine feel with some interesting plants in the summer.* At the bottom as the path turns sharp left, take a path RIGHT and follow it through woodland. There are

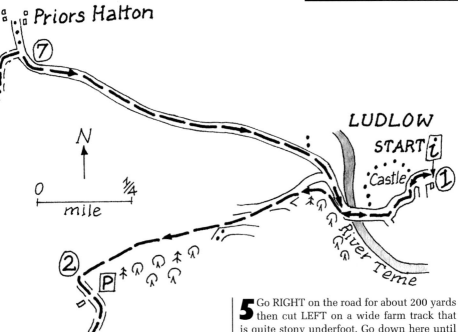

Priors Halton

LUDLOW
START

N

0 ¼ mile

a number of bird boxes here and you may spot a pied flycatcher if you are lucky. Also you may catch the spinning coin call of an unseen wood warbler from high in the canopy. The path continues to rise and passes through a gate. The fine field now on your left feels "secret" and often has deer in it. Continue to a field gate then keep to the right of the house until meeting a track. Turn LEFT and continue up to the road.

4 Turn RIGHT on the road, and in 100 yards cross with care to take the track LEFT. There are fine views towards Titterstone Clee, Wenlock Edge and Long Mynd from this high point. The track drops down and after a short distance there is a seat from which to appreciate the views in comfort. After resting, cross the wide stony track, continuing on the narrow path steeply down to a wide green track. Go through the metal gate ahead and descend through the field to a second gate onto a metalled road.

5 Go RIGHT on the road for about 200 yards then cut LEFT on a wide farm track that is quite stony underfoot. Go down here until you come to a crossing where there are number of gateways into fields. Take the path RIGHT and follow with the field boundary that has some fine oak trees along it on your left. It curves to the left and when you go through a gateway into the next field turn sharp RIGHT and follow now with a hedge on your right to the bottom of the field. Now turn LEFT along the stream until the bridge RIGHT after about 300 yards. This can be hidden when the trees are in full leaf so take care not to miss it.

6 Once over the bridge turn LEFT to the wire fence ahead. Turn RIGHT following this field boundary, again along the edge of a stream, until a gate takes you onto a farm track. Go LEFT here and follow the track until it joins the metalled road. This is Priors Halton – *a small community based around the farm on a no through road, although it boasts a pillar box!*

7 Turn RIGHT along the road and follow this quiet lane back to Ludlow. On the way you will get fine views of the Castle, and pass the organic Wigley's Field allotments and the Cliffe Hotel.

BURWAY CIRCULAR

DESCRIPTION A river plain route of 6 easy miles around the River Teme from Ludlow passing the Millennium Green and Green Cafe that provides excellent refreshment before or after the walk. The walk features Oakley Park, passes near to the Clive and Ludlow Food Centre, and Ludlow Racecourse. In wet weather the underpass at Bromfield can be flooded and great care is needed crossing the A49 road.

START & FINISH Ludlow Market Square, Visitor Information Centre SO 510746.

DIRECTIONS Ludlow is easily reached by bus or train, and the Market Square with castle gates is the town's meeting point. There is a Market Square car park nearby although it is far better to use the Park and Ride bus service from the Eco Park on the bypass. The route heads down behind the castle to the River Teme that loops round the town.

I With your back to the Visitor Information Centre go LEFT towards Ludlow Castle. Take Dinham, the road to the left of the Castle which drops down to the Millennium Green. Continue over Dinham Bridge over the River Teme, then when it heads up a hill to the left, go RIGHT into Halton Lane. Just before the entrance to the Cliffe Hotel turn RIGHT through a gate. This is the route of the Shropshire Way now; you'll be returning on the old route. Aim half LEFT across the field then descend steeply to cross a stream and two stiles. Climb again and follow the path above the river. Cross a stile straight ahead and continue around the edge of this field. The field narrows; go LEFT here across to cross a stile. Head down hill over the stream. Then aim LEFT up the edge of the field a short way then RIGHT on the clear path across the middle of the field. Proceed through a gate, follow the field boundary LEFT to cross another stile, then go LEFT soon to rejoin Halton Lane.

2 Turn RIGHT on the road, through a gate by a lodge then down the dip and up again. *This is Oakley Park Estate, a great area to see birds, and in spring the dip is covered in a superb carpet of marsh marigolds.* Continue straight on ignoring the road from left, passing over the River Teme where there's a hydro power project – *the weirs have been restored in the process. Look out for dippers and wagtails here, and possibly even otters, or at least otter footprints.* Continue to the gateway and entrance to the church – *at one time a priory until the Dissolution. There are also remains of a house built at this time by Charles Foxe who was a key figure in the Council of Wales based in Ludlow!* Join the pavement and then just before you reach the A49 take the subway path sharp RIGHT. Emerging on the opposite side head LEFT towards the Clive bistro, but go LEFT on the side road; continue ahead with care over the level crossing. Turn immediately RIGHT with the railway to the right and racecourse buildings left. At the B road go RIGHT over the railway to the junction with the A49. Cross with great care and head into the field opposite.

3 With the woodland to the right drop down the field then go LEFT with the hedge on your right. This is the old route of the Shropshire Way. Go through a gate and cross the grass area in front of a house. Continue past farm buildings and then through a gate. Follow this track, crossing a driveway, then onward in the same direction with the playing fields left. Pass though a gateway joining a track which soon becomes metalled, past houses on your right and the cricket club on your left. At the main road go RIGHT – this is Coronation Drive. After a few yards turn RIGHT at the gate into the field, following the well worn path, through a metal gate and onward to a wooden gate and bridge across the Corve just above a weir. When the path joins the road turn RIGHT through a gate into the Linney. (In times of flood miss out this section following Coronation Drive to a junction and RIGHT into the top of Linney down to the bend where the path joins). Continue ahead along Linney passing the tennis and bowling clubs on the right until the Millennium Green is reached, then back uphill to where you started.

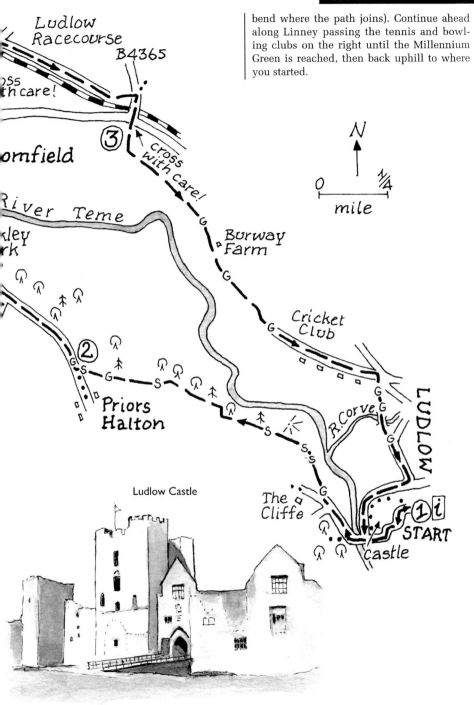

Ludlow Racecourse
B4365

oss
th care!

omfield

③ cross with care!

River Teme
ley
rk

Burway
Farm

Cricket
Club

② Priors
Halton

Ludlow Castle

The Cliffe

R.Corve

LUDLOW

START
Castle

N

0 ——— ¼
mile

WALK 5

RICHARD'S CASTLE TO LUDLOW

DESCRIPTION A great 6½ mile strenuous walk over the top of Mortimer Forest at High Vinnals that includes a bus ride from Ludlow Market Square to Richard's Castle. The route back is via The Goggin (could well be out of Lord of the Rings) and Hanway Common before climbing over the big hill, thus avoiding trudging with the modern pilgrimage from forestry car parks on forestry tracks to this well-known viewpoint. The walk includes sections of the Mortimer Trail, an exceptional walking route from Ludlow to Kington established in 1996.
START Richards Castle, Castle Inn SO 496695.
FINISH Ludlow Market Square SO 510746.
DIRECTIONS The walk really starts in Ludlow at the 492 bus stop by the Assembly Rooms in Mill Street just round the corner from the Market Square. There are regular buses in the week and three on Sundays and Bank Holidays. Alight from the bus on the B4361 in the dip at Richard's Castle, opposite the Castle Inn.

1 Take the road opposite the bus-stop next to the Castle Inn. This climbs steadily passing an interesting 17thC dovecote in the grounds of Court House Farm. Keep ahead at a junction and at the top of the hill turn LEFT as the road bends right, following the sign to the historic, but now redundant church of St Bartholomew. *The tower stands alongside the church; the remains of the castle can be reached from the church grounds.* Make the detour to enjoy this historic site.

2 After visiting the church and castle continue ahead on the footpath through two metal gates to join a farm track. Turn RIGHT and follow the track across a stream and then through a number of gates until you reach the top of the track into a field with fine views left to the

Goggin. Keep to the hedge on your right and follow it along the field to a gate.

3 Turn RIGHT on to the Mortimer Trail, walking along the grass track between two fields until the edge of Hanway common is reached. Go through the gate to the immediate left of the sheepfold and follow the path along the edge of the hedge onto the common. After a while the path keeps straight on as the hedge bears off to the left. After crossing a metalled track to the farm you will come across a seat. *Take a moment to look at the fine views of Titterstone Clee, Abberley and, in the distance, the Malverns.* The path now curves round to the left and through a gate into Mortimer Forest.

4 Continue along the track, ignoring the Herefordshire Trail on your left, until you join a large forestry track immediately beyond a black metal barrier. Turn LEFT and then immediately RIGHT and follow this track to the top of High Vinnals. *There's an old shooting box at the summit as well as a suitably positioned seat to take in the fine view towards Wales.*

5 Return to the main path from the seat and take the small path immediately in front of you signed Climbing Jack. This takes you over the common with views of Ludlow in the distance. Follow the path down crossing several forestry tracks. The signs change from Climbing Jack to Black Pool Loop and Mortimer Trail but when you reach a grass crossroads turn LEFT and pick up the Climbing Jack signs again. This path takes you down to a stream – turn LEFT when you reach the main forestry track and then after 10 yards RIGHT; cross and walk alongside the stream until you join another large forestry road.

6 Turn half LEFT and keep on the forestry road that sweeps in a right-hand curve past the old quarry faces, heading uphill. Where the road turns sharp left carry straight on to a smaller track where there is a metal gate which is almost always open. Follow this clear track past the isolated house known as Starvecrow until you reach a junction of paths. Take the path LEFT. After a few yards you will find a noticeboard that tells you about the old turnpike road from Leominster to Ludlow that you are now walking.

7 Continue ahead through a field and then through a kissing gate where you will be alongside the boundary of the house known as Mabbit's Horn, which also alludes to the coaching era. When you reach the road turn LEFT and walk down the pavement for about a quarter of a mile – it is a busy road so take care. When you reach the road junction on the RIGHT cross and walk down it past a number of

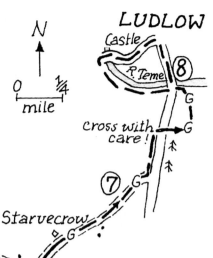

houses. At the end there are farm gates and despite the sign that says 'No Access' to the track, go through the gate and turn immediately LEFT along the pedestrian right of way that follows the edge of a field, finally reaching a kissing gate that takes you onto a small road with a garden of remembrance on your right hand side.

8 When you reach the end of the road, opposite the Charlton Arms, you can turn RIGHT, cross Ludford Bridge and then walk up the hill through the Broad Street arch to the Buttercross in the centre of Ludlow. Alternatively you can cross straight over and walk up the road signposted Wigmore for a few yards. Then take the steps up RIGHT and follow the path until it leads to the Breadwalk alongside the Teme. This will take you to Dinham Bridge and the Green Cafe. From here it's RIGHT up Dinham to the market square in the centre of Ludlow.

WALK 6

CLEE HILL TO LUDLOW (ECO PARK)

DESCRIPTION This 5 mile moderate linear walk offers splendid views across South Shropshire to Ludlow. It starts at Clee Hill, a community which is closely associated with quarrying and descends to the quiet hamlet of Knowbury before following the old Shropshire Way route back to the Eco Park. There is a coffee shop at Swifts Bakery in Clee Hill, and the walk passes by the Bennetts End Inn at Knowbury.

START Clee Hill, Swifts Bakery SO 593754.

FINISH Ludlow, Eco Park SO 529744.

DIRECTIONS The start of the walk is on the 292 bus route between Ludlow, Cleobury Mortimer and Kidderminster. It runs 2 hourly on Mondays to Saturdays from the top of Corve Street (near Compasses Inn).

lar direction in the next field to the brow, but then change direction; cut LEFT to the bottom left corner where you join a bridleway. Clee Hill has many paths and bridleways which would have, at one time, been pathways to work for those involved in timber production, quarrying or small scale mining.

2 Proceed on the bridleway through a gate and then through two more gates. The path narrows and runs through scrub to exit at a stile on the RIGHT (ignore the one on the left). Go LEFT to descend to the bottom of the field and ignore stiles to the left and ahead, instead go RIGHT to follow the hedge on the left to a tree lined track. Part way along go LEFT over a stile and head slightly RIGHT down the field to climb two stiles in the far bottom right corner onto the road. Turn RIGHT to pass the Bennetts End Inn; it's too tempting to pass by this traditional hostelry so step inside for a while.

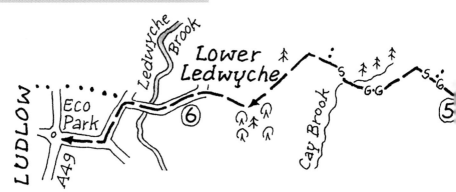

I From the entrance to Swifts Bakery shop and café turn LEFT and LEFT again but within a few paces cross the Tenbury Road to go through a small gate. Go ahead on a path running between gardens. Go through a second gate, over the road and the path soon drops down steps to a lane. Go over and walk ahead with a dwelling to your left. Cross a stile to enter a field. Keep ahead at first and through a remnant of a hedge then onward to cross a stile and tractor track. Keep in a simi-

3 From the entrance to the Bennett's End Inn, go LEFT to walk up road through Knowbury village. The road bends LEFT and continues ahead (ignore tracks and roads off) to a staggered crossroads with the Caynham Road. Cross over and head in the direction of Snitton for about half a mile. The road dips by cottages and soon after it begins to descend again and bends to the right. Look for a stile and waymark post on the left, signposted Shropshire Way. There's a sumptuous view of Ludlow from here.

12

4 Cross the stile, but ignore the stile ahead as you leave the 'new' Shropshire Way to follow the line of the old route. Go ahead down to the bottom corner and cross a stile into the next field. Follow the hedge on the left ahead and as it bends left keep ahead to cross a stile to the right of a gate. Keep ahead again in the next field and go over a stile and footbridge. Proceed ahead to go over a stile and footbridge in the next hedge. Continue ahead with the hedge on the left and at the bottom cut RIGHT to go through a gateway on the left. Continue ahead to reach a junction of tracks at the bottom of the field.

5 Turn RIGHT to cross a stile by a gate and down the track, across a junction of tracks and ahead through a gate. Go ahead to cross a stile by a gate into a long field. Head slightly LEFT across it to a gate. Go through here and cut half RIGHT to pass through a gate. Aim slightly LEFT to descend towards the Cay brook which is crossed by a bridge. Head slightly LEFT to cross another stile by a gate. Go ahead alongside the hedge to your left. In the field corner go slightly LEFT over a little bridge and then ahead again with a hedge to your left. At the junction by the wood, turn LEFT and continue along the track which curves RIGHT through a wood and ahead once again in the next field. Continue ahead to reach the road in Ledwyche, a hamlet that at one time nestled around a mill.

6 Go LEFT to follow the lane over the River Ledwyche and then LEFT up to Street. Cross over onto the pavement at the junction and turn RIGHT for a short walk to the turning for the Eco Park. The bus stop for town is on the RIGHT. If you prefer to walk into Ludlow (rather than catching the bus) then follow instruction 7 in Walk 2.

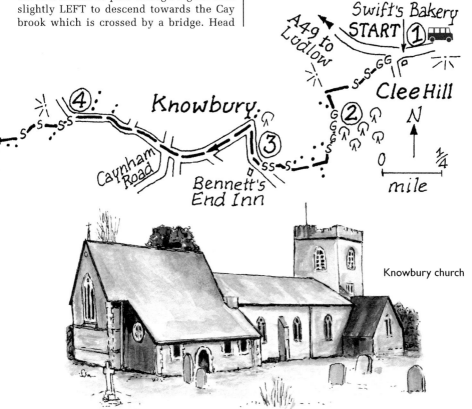

Knowbury church

WALK 7

TITTERSTONE CLEE HILL CIRCULAR

DESCRIPTION Titterstone Clee Hill with its sharp scarp edge and radar dome dominates the skyline around Ludlow. This excellent strenuous 7½ mile walk from Clee Hill village first skirts the hill as it passes a working quarry, heads over open access moorland, drops to a pretty hamlet before finally heading up steeply to the summit. The return takes in a strange lunar landscape past the radome then old quarry-workings before dropping down the old quarry incline eventually returning through quarry villages to base. The Titterstone Clee Heritage Trust does much good work to conserve this landscape which has fascinated for centuries; it is after all the only hill to be named on the 14thC Mappa Mundi housed at Hereford Cathedral. There is a coffee shop at Swifts Bakery in Clee Hill village and two pubs to take refreshment.

START & FINISH Clee Hill Village SO 593754.

DIRECTIONS The start of the walk is the stop for the 292 bus route between Ludlow, Cleobury Mortimer and Kidderminster. The bus runs 2-hourly on Mondays to Saturdays. There's a small car park at the top of the village.

I From the bus stop in the centre of the village walk up ahead to the car park on the right just before the cattle grid. From the top corner of the car park there is a path parallel to the road that leads to the toposcope with fine views to the east, south and west. From the toposcope walk towards the road and cross by the house called Craven Place – this used to be the offices for the quarries. Follow the road for about ½ mile that leads alongside the current quarry workings taking care to keep to the side of the road (there's a green verge guarded by rocks for most of the way) as it is well used by lorries going to the quarry. Do not take either a left turn into the works or a right turn down to the main road.

2 The track rises to the right to a fork on the open land. Take the LEFT fork at a sign for Random Farm. Soon you will catch a glimpse of a stark dead tree on the skyline; that is where you will be heading. After 300 yards, as the road curves left and straightens alongside a wide green verge, a well marked grass track crosses the road. Turn LEFT onto this open access track and follow it as it heads uphill and then bears right to pass the dead tree. Immediately past the tree head LEFT on the small grass path and soon you will see the fence ahead of you. Head downhill through the rocks toward the copse of trees in front of you and you will meet a larger track that heads through this area of grass and reeds. Turn LEFT on to this path and follow it diagonally down to the far corner of the intake fence where several tracks meet.

3 Now follow the path which bends to the right, away from the radomes, and meanders near to the field boundary on your right. Keep to this path until the hedge cuts right. You keep slighly left here on a less distinct track to join another fence. Follow this and pick up a track again which weaves its way down the hillside near the fence on the right; there are good views to the north. *As it drops down you will see the church in Cleeton St Mary, which is where you are heading next. There are a good number of grassland birds in this area and if you walk in spring/early summer you may hear curlew – this is one of the last places in Shropshire that they breed.*

4 Take time to look at the church and then go RIGHT along the road to the bus shelter (complete with a sheep gate). Turn sharp LEFT on the road that doubles back behind the church and follow it as far as Cleetongate – a house on the right. Now go LEFT directed by the bridleway sign. The track follows the fence on your right. Follow this for about a mile. After a while the fence becomes an attractive hedge with a number of native trees and some fine young holly trees.

5 At Callowgate, a house on your right, ease away from the hedge on the right to a waymark post. This is the junction where you meet the Shropshire Way and head LEFT for the clear path going up to the summit of Clee Hill, aiming just to the right of the larger radome. It reaches a point where you bear RIGHT up a steep climb so take time to stop and turn round and enjoy the views to Brown Clee and beyond. At the top the Shropshire Way heads to the right and to a trig point. Now continue to follow the Shropshire Way signs along the top of the old quarry past the radomes. You can see the large car park on your right and this is where you are heading but you need to follow the track straight ahead for a while before it turns right and drops down to the road.

6 Turn LEFT on the road and then after 100 yards on the track RIGHT. This takes you to the old ruined quarry buildings. Now by the third building on your right look out for the Shropshire Way sign that sends you LEFT gently down the old cable hauled railway known as the Titterstone Incline. Follow the incline until you reach a bridge over a track – there is a sign showing you the way LEFT down to the track that passes under the old trackbed. *Spend a moment looking at the fine stonework in this old bridge.* At the bottom of the steps you'll be facing back up the incline; turn RIGHT and follow the clear track past a house and over a small road.

7 The path now crosses a footbridge over a stream and then curves to the right and up to a gate. Go through the gate and carry straight on to go through the field gate directly in front of you by a house. Turn RIGHT and follow this track uphill, through a gate and then to the right when it eventually joins a minor road. Turn RIGHT and walk down through Dhustone village – *noting old quarrymen's cottages in Rouse Boughton Terrace as well as Hedgehog House which is the home of the British Hedgehog Preservation Society.* Continue down the road for about 300 yards and after going over an old bridge, go LEFT onto a track past the house call Rockleigh. Go through the gate ahead and carry straight on along the old railway trackbed with more old quarry buildings on your left. This path continues until it goes past the back of hous-

es in Clee Hill village and joins a small road via a metal gate where the Kremlin public house can be seen on the left. Turn RIGHT and go over the cattle grid to join the main road where you started.

WALK 8

ONIBURY CIRCULAR

DESCRIPTION This walk of 7½ miles from the hamlet of Onibury heads over fields and byways up to the hill fortress at Norton Camp, then swoops down into the Onny valley to Stokesay Castle before returning back through mixed countryside to the start. Refreshment is available at the Apple Tree, Onibury and there's a tea room at Stokesay Castle for visitors.

START & FINISH Onibury, Apple Tree pub SO 453792.

DIRECTIONS Easy access is by the 435 bus from Ludlow (Mons-Sats) that stops in the lay-by just north of Onibury level crossing, where the A49 can be crossed. Walk up the side road past Onibury Village Hall towards the Apple Tree pub, which used to be a Post Office and General Stores. It is well worth a visit and makes a good starting-point for this walk. There is limited parking on the road by the church or at the village hall.

1 At the junction before the pub go RIGHT, walking past school and church with its magnificent cedar tree. At the end of the housing turn LEFT on an un-signed track. Just before going into the yard at the top of the track go RIGHT into the field and then immediately LEFT to walk up the field.

2 Cross a stile at the top and continue along the edge of the field with Oakern Rookery on your left. There are good views of Clee Hill and Brown Clee. Cross the double stile just past the farm gate at the top of the field and continue with a hedge on your left. After another stile go straight across the field to the stile opposite. Continue in the same direction across the field. Go through the gate and then head slightly RIGHT across a bridge over a stream. There is a lake on your left. Walk up the field close to the hedge until you go RIGHT over stile after about 100 yards then HALF LEFT to cross the stile over the fence.

3 Head HALF RIGHT towards the farm buildings. There is a stile through a hedge

and a piece of wire to get under before joining the track towards the farm. Follow it toward the barns ignore the metal gate on the left. At the end of the track go LEFT through a gate into the yard then turn RIGHT to walk ahead between buildings; follow the track for about ½ mile going through six gates and curving gently left. You will see houses on your right; the track is less distinct but with a hedge still to your left. Keep ahead to cross the fifth gate; just before the final gate onto the road there's a pond on the right.

4 Turn right on the road past a house then go LEFT on the track. After 20 yards turn LEFT through a gate and follow the path around the back of the house. There is another gate then head across the field towards the farm ahead.. Cross a fence stile by a gate into the next field and then head straight up the field keeping the long barn on your right. Go through the gates into the farmyard with disused barns on your right and through the green gate on to the road at Norton.

5 Cross the road onto the waymarked path that bears left through scrub. Emerge by a gate bearing RIGHT onto a track and climb uphill with views behind towards Clee Hill. After a little over half a mile the track turns right. Continue up here until you reach the house at the top at Norton Camp.

6 Go RIGHT by the red brick outbuilding and follow the track through rhododendrons obscuring the earthworks of the hill-fort. Look out for a footpath straight ahead when the main track turns left, just before a cage to farmed pheasants. The path is not clear at this point. Follow it through the large cherry laurels to join the larger path that turns left and follows the slope of the hill downwards. Ignore the turnings off left and right and also the first marked footpath that heads across a field. Instead continue along a track through attractive beech and oak woods. After the track turns right take the sunken track RIGHT between two fields down to the road.

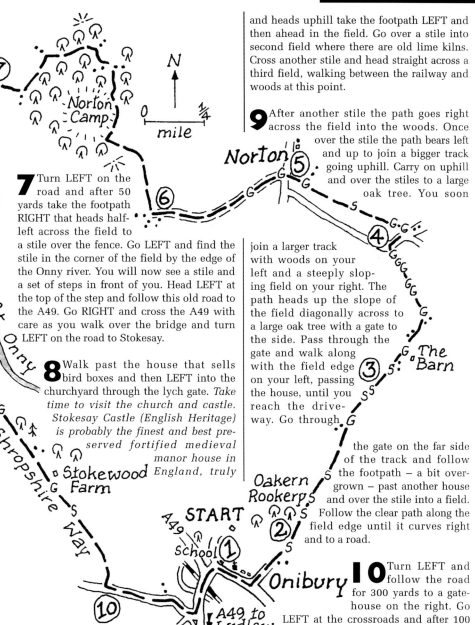

and heads uphill take the footpath LEFT and then ahead in the field. Go over a stile into second field where there are old lime kilns. Cross another stile and head straight across a third field, walking between the railway and woods at this point.

9 After another stile the path goes right across the field into the woods. Once over the stile the path bears left and up to join a bigger track going uphill. Carry on uphill and over the stiles to a large oak tree. You soon join a larger track with woods on your left and a steeply sloping field on your right. The path heads up the slope of the field diagonally across to a large oak tree with a gate to the side. Pass through the gate and walk along with the field edge on your left, passing the house, until you reach the driveway. Go through the gate on the far side of the track and follow the footpath – a bit overgrown – past another house and over the stile into a field. Follow the clear path along the field edge until it curves right and to a road.

7 Turn LEFT on the road and after 50 yards take the footpath RIGHT that heads half-left across the field to a stile over the fence. Go LEFT and find the stile in the corner of the field by the edge of the Onny river. You will now see a stile and a set of steps in front of you. Head LEFT at the top of the step and follow this old road to the A49. Go RIGHT and cross the A49 with care as you walk over the bridge and turn LEFT on the road to Stokesay.

8 Walk past the house that sells bird boxes and then LEFT into the churchyard through the lych gate. *Take time to visit the church and castle. Stokesay Castle (English Heritage) is probably the finest and best preserved fortified medieval manor house in England, truly borderland architecture.* Leave the castle and church using the gate opposite the car park and go LEFT on a road past farm buildings and houses to cross the railway with care. Follow the track but when it curves right

10 Turn LEFT and follow the road for 300 yards to a gatehouse on the right. Go LEFT at the crossroads and after 100 yards, join the A49. Turn LEFT and then cross the road with care before the level crossing. There is a pedestrian bridge over the river next to the road bridge. You are now back in Onibury with perhaps time to call into the Apple Tree.

17

CRAVEN ARMS TO WISTANSTOW

DESCRIPTION This easy 7 mile walk starts from the Shropshire Hills Discovery Centre, Craven Arms home to Grow, Cook and Learn, a social enterprise focusing on the local food economy. You will pass by Woods brewery tap, the Plough and the Smithy shop at Wistanstow and Strefford Hall where there's a farm shop; all these sell local produce and the walk illustrates where our food comes from.

START & FINISH Shropshire Hills Discovery Centre, Craven Arms SO 436325.

DIRECTIONS Craven Arms is well served by trains from Ludlow daily; it is a 10 minute walk through town to the Discovery Centre. The 435 Ludlow to Shrewsbury bus stops just by Market Street, the turning for the Discovery Centre; it operates hourly Mondays to Fridays and two hourly on Saturdays. There is car parking available at the Centre.

1 From the entrance to the Discovery Centre, go through the car park to a small gateway and cross Market Street. Go LEFT and at the junction cross the A49 road using the Pelican crossing. Go LEFT and then first RIGHT along Dodd's Lane, keeping ahead through housing onto a track, under a railway bridge and then cross a stile by a gate to enter a field. Go ahead at first by three trees then slightly RIGHT to cross a stile into the next pasture. Aim slightly RIGHT to climb another stile and join the boundary with the Heart of Wales railway. Follow this ahead to a stile by a gate and onward to another into Watling Street, an old Roman road.

2 Go right along the road, under the railway bridge then cross the B road to Clun. Go RIGHT and LEFT to continue on Watling Street to rise up and then look for a stile on the left before a house. This is the Shropshire Way. Cross it and walk ahead on a tractor track to pass through a kissing gate and proceed ahead to climb a stile at the next boundary. Part way along the hedge

on the left cross a stile and turn right for 50 yards or so, then slightly LEFT over a plank bridge and stile. Go RIGHT on the lane which is very quiet. It is about half a mile to a crossroads where you continue ahead for another half a mile to a second crossroads.

3 Go ahead to walk along a track which descends beneath the old trackbed of the Bishop's Castle Railway, which closed in 1939. This section can be wet in the rainy season so take care to walk alongside a stream to a footbridge over the Onny and up to a main road. Cross over and walk up the hill to Wistanstow village. Go LEFT at the junction to pass the Plough and ahead to Holy Trinity church, a grade II listed building. Go through the lych gate, turn RIGHT and LEFT in the churchyard then ahead through the graveyard and by monuments to an outer cemetery. Head for the far right corner where there's a kissing gate into a field.

4 Walk along the hedge on the left, through a gate and over a footbridge. Go ahead, cross a stile in the next boundary and aim slightly right between two trees. At the hedge, go right and then aim slightly right to cross a stile, the railway tracks and another stile. *Be careful.* Follow the hedge ahead to two barred gates and a short track to the A49 road. Cross with care and walk down to Strefford Hall. There's a farm shop is to the right and free range eggs are available at the farm itself. Turn RIGHT at the next junction in the hamlet of Strefford; this gives out at a gate into a field. Walk along the tractor track; as it bends right keep ahead, through a bridle gate and ahead along a fence to another. Once through continue by the Quinny Brook to a cross a footbridge over it.

5 Go ahead to cross another bridge on the right. Head very slightly RIGHT, cross a stile and ahead by the side of two fields to reach a gate at Berrymill cottage. Continue ahead along a track, cross a stile, follow a field path slightly RIGHT to a gate into a wood. Cross a stile into a pasture, then ahead through a gateway now with a hedge to the left to reach a top corner. Cross a stile and turn RIGHT to cross two more onto a road. Continue ahead through Halford to the B4368.

6 At the junction go RIGHT but before the bridge cross over and go through a gate. The path cuts left and then slightly RIGHT across a water meadow to a footbridge. Go over this and continue ahead by houses to pass the community gardens, and to the left the Onny Meadows, to the Discovery Centre.

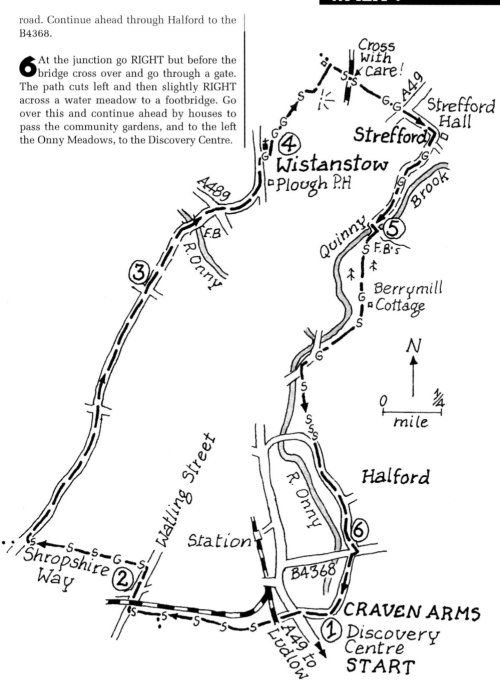

BROOME
TO HOPESAY

DESCRIPTION A moderate walk of 6 miles that takes in a wonderful flood-plain section by the River Clun to Aston on Clun then heads up to a common high on Hopesay Hill before returning through pleasant glades to Aston and thence back to Broome. The Shropshire Hills Area of Outstanding Natural Beauty has worked with partners to improve the river habitats of the Clun, including coppicing alders and seeking to encourage colonies of the rare and declining pearl mussels found in the river. Refreshment is available at Glebe Farm in Hopesay, the Kangaroo Inn and at the Community shop (teas, coffees and snacks available) both in Aston on Clun. The bridleway between Hopesay and Aston is often waterlogged in winter so be prepared to get wet feet.

START & FINISH Broome Railway Station SO 399809.

DIRECTIONS The walk starts at Broome Station accessed by the magnificent Heart of Wales railway line, a stubborn survivor in an era where growth and speed are the modern mantras. Limited parking is also available near the station.

I From the station in Broome head for B4369 road where you turn LEFT towards Aston on Clun. After about 250 yards follow the footpath sign LEFT over a stile and walk diagonally across the field, crossing a stile onto a metalled drive. Go LEFT along it towards the bridge over the Clun. Before the river go RIGHT over the stile. Take the track over the smaller stream but first admire this wonderful view of the River Clun. Head roughly quarter RIGHT to the stile on the opposite side of the field. Cross, then immediately go through a gate and along the farm track towards the houses. After another gate you will be on the obviously named Redwood Drive and this leads to the B4368 road through Aston on Clun. The Kangaroo pub is on your right. Turn LEFT, cross the road with care and head to the famous Arbor Tree in the centre of the village. *The flags*

on the Arbor Tree are renewed annually at the end of May to celebrate the marriage of Squire Marston of Oaker to Mary Carter of Sibdon in 1786.

2 From the Arbor tree walk RIGHT up Mill Street alongside the stream. Notice the sign on the old Baptist chapel on your right. The road turns left at the top and the footpath is signposted here. After passing some bungalows on your left go through the gate in front of you (with a post box) and a clear footpath sign. Walk up the driveway for 200 yards. The drive continues steeply but the footpath bears slightly LEFT past a telegraph pole. This is a broad grassy path with the River Clun well below on the left. At a marker post by some gorse bushes take the LEFT fork and keep ahead on the level path. Bear RIGHT at the next marker post and when the gorse hedge on your right finishes continue walking on the same level round the top of some trees that are below on your left. Carry straight on and go into the mixed birch and beech woods by the corner of a post and wire fence. Continue with the wire fence on your right and cross over the stile to take you out of the woodland. The path is clearly marked, and once you have crossed the next stile, follow the path down to the left across the wooden footbridge onto a metalled track.

3 Turn RIGHT then immediately LEFT by a house and follow the path until you come to two gates. Go through the gate on the RIGHT and then after about 20 yards take a clear grassy path leading up to the top of Hopesay Hill. *Near the top there is a welcome seat on the left that is an ideal spot for lunch or just to appreciate the views. Look out for red kites above the hill – they are quite common here now. This is also a good spot for a wide variety of fungi and if you are lucky you'll see the ponies roaming wild across the common.* Leaving the seat head for the top of the hill and then head slightly down to the walkers' signpost at the col saddle in front of you. The paths go in a number of directions here and you are looking for the one signed Hopesay Village and Clun, ie, turning back on yourself. This is a clear path hard to the north (RIGHT) of the one that you came from; look for a distinct grey barn in the distance ahead. The path descends through bracken to a gate at the bottom of the hillside (just to the left,). Go through it to join the road and pass a farm. At the T-junction turn LEFT and again turn LEFT at the next junction to go into Hopesay village *This belonged to Picot de Say in Norman times, hence the name meaning a valley of the Say family.* After 100 yards there is a road on the right that leads to the church *– where it is possible to see many early Norman features –* and also the tea-room at Hopesay Glebe Farm (which is open Friday to Monday but check times in winter).

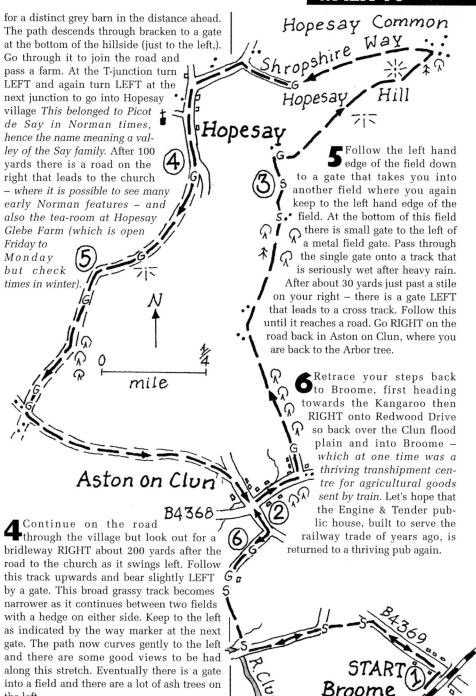

5 Follow the left hand edge of the field down to a gate that takes you into another field where you again keep to the left hand edge of the field. At the bottom of this field there is small gate to the left of a metal field gate. Pass through the single gate onto a track that is seriously wet after heavy rain. After about 30 yards just past a stile on your right – there is a gate LEFT that leads to a cross track. Follow this until it reaches a road. Go RIGHT on the road back in Aston on Clun, where you are back to the Arbor tree.

6 Retrace your steps back to Broome, first heading towards the Kangaroo then RIGHT onto Redwood Drive so back over the Clun flood plain and into Broome – *which at one time was a thriving transhipment centre for agricultural goods sent by train.* Let's hope that the Engine & Tender public house, built to serve the railway trade of years ago, is returned to a thriving pub again.

4 Continue on the road through the village but look out for a bridleway RIGHT about 200 yards after the road to the church as it swings left. Follow this track upwards and bear slightly LEFT by a gate. This broad grassy track becomes narrower as it continues between two fields with a hedge on either side. Keep to the left as indicated by the way marker at the next gate. The path now curves gently to the left and there are some good views to be had along this stretch. Eventually there is a gate into a field and there are a lot of ash trees on the left.

21

BUCKNELL CIRCULAR

DESCRIPTION A moderate 4 mile walk climbing through Bucknell Wood before descending to a place called Cubbat and returning along Daffodil lane into the village. Many of these paths have been cleared by the local walking group, Bucknell Walkers, which has done an exceptionally good job of maintaining rights of way in the parish; there are also a number of other longer walks available by looking at bucknellwalkers.blogspot.com. Refreshment can be found at the Sitwell Arms or at the Baron at Bucknell and there are two shops.

START & FINISH Railway Station, Bucknell SO 355737.

DIRECTIONS Start the walk at Bucknell Railway Station on the Heart of Wales railway line (daily service). The 738/740 bus from Ludlow also stops here, four buses per day on Mondays to Saturdays and in the summer the Castle Connect (783) also stops here on Saturdays and Sundays. There is limited on street parking near to Bucknell railway station.

I From the entrance to the railway station go LEFT to cross the tracks, and then RIGHT along the B4367 road to pass by the Sitwell Arms and by Greens Garage. Just after, turn LEFT as signposted to walk along a track which soon bends left to a dwelling. However, you keep ahead through two gates and onward along fencing to a third gate onto a track. *The scant earthworks of Bucknell castle are nearby. It was built not long after 1066 by Ralph de Mortimer under the stewardship of Roger Montgomery II, important lords who gave loyal support to William the Conqueror.* Continue ahead along the track and at the road turn RIGHT to follow the main street as it bends left and then ahead. Pass by the entrance to the Baron public house and then take the next RIGHT turn, Bridgend Lane.

2 Follow this to a point where a road at Seabridge Meadow dips down to a ford.

Go LEFT here but you are in luck as there's a footbridge too. Cross the road to walk up the bridleway which leads to Bucknell Wood. At the junction turn RIGHT on a forestry track by a barrier. This rises to a junction by an old quarry. Go LEFT and then RIGHT through a gate but then within 15 yards cut LEFT to climb up the hillside in a sunken lane. This can get tricky as there are often fallen branches across the line of route but persevere until the path levels and reaches a junction with a wider forestry track.

3 Ignore the track immediately left and descend on the main track which curves left to run between tall conifers and patches of deciduous trees. At the junction, as the main track bends left, keep ahead to a second junction in approximately 50 yards. Go RIGHT here and drop down the road at Cubbat, ignoring tracks off to the right or left on the way. At the road, go LEFT. This descends at first then bends left as well as rising gently. Go LEFT through a double gate and make your way slightly LEFT across the pasture to a barred gate, and once through, rise up and ahead with the wood to the right. At the top, go through a gate and wet ground into a field. Proceed very slightly RIGHT to cross a stile.

4 Go LEFT and then RIGHT at a junction to drop down the hillside on tractor tracks which becomes Daffodil Lane. This reaches the main road by an amenity ground on the left. At the junction, keep ahead for about 30 yards. Go through a gate on the RIGHT. The path bends to the left and through a kissing gate into the next field. Go ahead towards Bucknell church with a view of Coxall Knoll behind and Brampton Park to the right in the distance. *Bucknell church is thought to date from the 12thC but was completely revamped in the 1860s as were many churches in Victorian times. However, the font is thought to be early Norman or some suggest early Saxon, thus there may well have been an earlier church on the same site.* Continue ahead through another kissing gate. Now head slightly right and then to the left to exit onto a road through a kissing gate. Cross with care. Go LEFT and then RIGHT to walk on

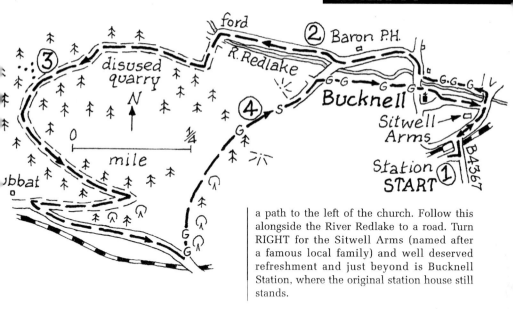

a path to the left of the church. Follow this alongside the River Redlake to a road. Turn RIGHT for the Sitwell Arms (named after a famous local family) and well deserved refreshment and just beyond is Bucknell Station, where the original station house still stands.

Bucknell railway station

LEINTWARDINE CIRCULAR

DESCRIPTION This 6 mile moderate walk offers the walker superb views over the Teme Valley, across the Wigmore Rolls and beyond to the Radnor Forest. It follows the Herefordshire Trail for the first part then along bridleways and through Mocktree. The walk is based on the Roman settlement of Leintwardine and a visit to the parish church is a must as there are several delightful misericord carvings in the Chancel stalls. The Victorian Parlour pub, the Sun Inn on Rosemary Lane is also a good place to finish the walk as it is offers a balanced combination of heritage and modernity but most of all a warm welcome.

START & FINISH Leintwardine village green opposite the Lion Hotel SO 404738.

DIRECTIONS The start of the walk is on the 738-740 bus route; the bus operates Mondays to Saturdays between Ludlow and Knighton. In addition there's a summer weekend service to Bishop's Castle (783), part of the Shropshire Shuttles network. There is a limited amount of on-road parking in the village.

I From the ancient tree on the green (there's a shelter underneath it), turn RIGHT along Rosemary Lane, then go LEFT into High Street. Pass the turning for the church on the left and just beyond go right along a dead end lane. Cross a stile ahead and go LEFT over a second stile and along the hedge on the left to yet another stile. Cross this and at the next corner keep slightly RIGHT to pass through a straggly hawthorn hedge and in a similar direction to cross a stile in the next boundary. Go slightly LEFT to a footbridge, then slightly LEFT again across a pasture to cross a stile onto a lane. Go RIGHT to walk through Kinton, a quiet hamlet, then LEFT at the junction to rise on a sunken lane to the A4113 road.

2 Cross the road with care. Go ahead on a track, ignore the bridleway off to the right; there's also a dwelling to the right. The track bends to the right. Before you reach a gate, go LEFT over a stile into a field. Aim slightly RIGHT to another stile. Once across head in a similar direction (slightly LEFT) to a thorn and hazel hedge where there's a waymark post to guide you. Duck under the branches and then go ahead in the next pasture to a gap in the hedge and fence crossing which leads to a track. Turn RIGHT to climb up the hillside, through a gateway and up again to a stile. Cross the stile, the path heads RIGHT across the field corner towards a tree. The path now bears slightly RIGHT across the field to the next stile. Keep ahead to cross another stile and in a similar direction up the next field to a junction of green tracks in at a hedge opening. There are great views from here across the Teme Valley to Wales and also up the Clun Valley to the right. You can just see Leintwardine in the foreground.

3 Go RIGHT here before the opening with a hedge to your left. Proceed through a gate and continue ahead to reach a junction. Keep ahead again and the track soon bends left at a place known as Far Barn (but the barn no longer exists). Just around the corner go RIGHT and walk ahead along a green strip amid open fields. This leads to a junction before a wood. There are superb views here across to Wenlock Edge and Brown Clee. Go hard RIGHT down the field edge with the woods on your left to follow a tractor track which becomes a main track for about half a mile, passing by a barn and eventually coming to a sharp bend to the right. Go LEFT here through the second gate and then RIGHT. Head slightly right across the field to the far right corner. Cross a stile and drop down (it is a drop too) to a lane. Go LEFT to walk down to a junction near Mocktree Barns Holiday Cottages.

4 Go RIGHT across the green verge and cross the main road with care. A private road runs ahead but your way is to the RIGHT, down a woodland track which winds its way down Coleswood. At the bottom of the wood, go through a barred gate and walk through the pasture near to the woodland on the left. Go through a gateway (the one

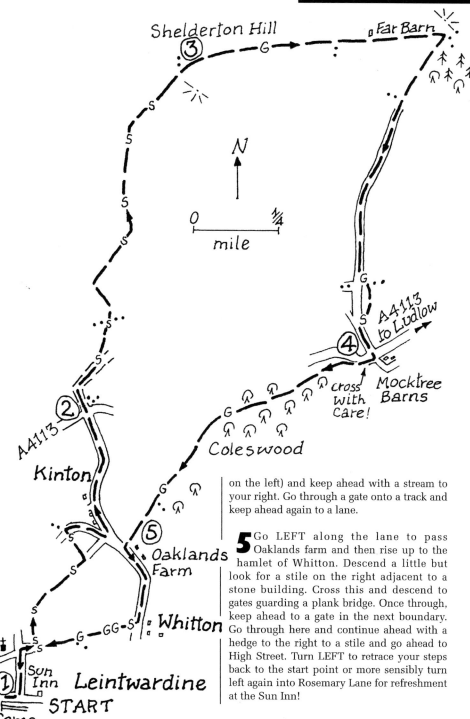

on the left) and keep ahead with a stream to your right. Go through a gate onto a track and keep ahead again to a lane.

5 Go LEFT along the lane to pass Oaklands farm and then rise up to the hamlet of Whitton. Descend a little but look for a stile on the right adjacent to a stone building. Cross this and descend to gates guarding a plank bridge. Once through, keep ahead to a gate in the next boundary. Go through here and continue ahead with a hedge to the right to a stile and go ahead to High Street. Turn LEFT to retrace your steps back to the start point or more sensibly turn left again into Rosemary Lane for refreshment at the Sun Inn!

LEINTWARDINE TO CRAVEN ARMS

DESCRIPTION A classy 7 mile linear walk with suitable transport connections from and back to Ludlow. It is worth every bit of the effort because of the superb views over Shelderton Hill and on View Edge, and it heads back into Craven Arms through one of the very best woods for bluebells and spring flowers. This is a walk through very quiet underrated Shropshire countryside.

START Village Green, Leintwardine SO 404738.

FINISH Craven Arms Railway Station SO 432831.

DIRECTIONS The start of the walk is on the 738-740 bus route; the bus operates Mondays to Saturdays between Ludlow and Knighton. In addition there's a summer weekend service to Bishop's Castle (783). There is a limited amount of on-road parking in the village.

I From the ancient tree on the green (there's a shelter underneath it), turn RIGHT along Rosemary Lane, then go LEFT into High Street. Pass the turning for the church on the left and just beyond go right along a dead end lane. Cross a stile ahead and go LEFT over a second stile and along the hedge to yet another stile. Cross this and at the next corner keep slightly RIGHT to pass through a straggly hawthorn hedge and in a similar direction to cross a stile in the next boundary. Go slightly LEFT to a footbridge, then slightly LEFT again across a pasture to cross a stile onto a lane. Go RIGHT to walk through the hamlet of Kinton then LEFT at the junction to rise on a sunken lane to the A4113 road.

2 Cross the road with care. Go ahead on a track, ignore the bridleway off to the right; there's dwelling to the right. The track bends to the right. Before you reach a gate, go LEFT over a stile into a field. Aim slightly RIGHT to another stile. Once across head in

a similar direction (slightly LEFT) to a thorn and hazel hedge where there's a waymark post to guide you. Duck under the branches and then go ahead in the next pasture to a gap in the hedge and fence crossing which leads to a track. Turn RIGHT to climb up the hillside, through a gateway and up again to a stile. Cross the stile, the path heads RIGHT across the field corner towards a tree. The path now bears slightly RIGHT across the field to the next stile. Keep ahead to cross another stile and in a similar direction up the next field to a junction of green tracks in at a hedge opening. *There are great views from here across the Teme Valley to Wales and also up the Clun Valley to the right. You can just see Leintwardine in the foreground.*

3 Now take the path waymarked on your left through the opening and follow it keeping the fence on your left. At the top of the field go RIGHT and soon cross the stile LEFT into the next field and turn immediately RIGHT. Walk along the side of this large field with the hedge on your right. When the path joins track turn LEFT down to cross the road at Shelderton Rock.

4 Go through the gateway and head very slightly RIGHT in large field to a gap in a remnant hedge. Continue ahead with a hedge to the left and step slightly RIGHT around a small pond on left. Now head slightly RIGHT to go over the stile then down through the field, through a gate, towards Brandhill Farm. Go through the gate to the right onto a short track and then turn LEFT at the road junction. Now turn almost immediately RIGHT down a track between hedges with a house on right. After about 200 yards, before a cottage, turn LEFT on a waymarked footpath, running alongside a hedge up a bank for about 100 yards. Cut LEFT to cross a stile and follow the hedge to your right across another stile. Continue through a barred gate to join a road.

5 Go RIGHT on road for about 300 yards until there is a large barn on left. Go LEFT along a track up to a barn, passing it on the right, through the yard and a double gate on a track. Go down the dip to a stile then up the hill in front of you. Go RIGHT at the gap and continue with a hedge on the right. Cross a stile, now open on the right and with woodland on left. Continue ahead, to cross another stile and until you climb a stile on to road at the top of View Edge escarpment. A short diversion down the road RIGHT will bring you to an old quarry on the left, an SSSI with special geological and botanical interest.

6 Go LEFT on road then immediately RIGHT along a waymarked path alongside a cottage garden. Follow the clearly marked path as it dips downhill along the edge of Edge Wood. After 300 yards the path bears slightly RIGHT back into the wood until emerging into a field corner. You will see a track below heading through a gate at this point. The footpath follows the woodland edge parallel with the track, crosses a stile, and then soon cuts LEFT down the bank just before the cottage. At the track turn RIGHT until the junction of paths at 'Clapping Wicket'.

7 Cross the stile and farm track then take the footpath over another stile heading diagonally half left across the field. Cross the stile and follow until you go RIGHT at the woodland edge, over a stile then LEFT over another stile into Sallow Coppice. Turn RIGHT on the permissive path always keeping the line of the field edge on your right. *During spring the Coppice is full of white wood anemones, bluebells and yellow archangel .... if you time it right they can all be found together.* Follow the path through the woods eventually downhill bearing RIGHT at path T-junction.

8 Follow the substantial path with hedge on left. Look out for a stile after 300 yards. Go LEFT taking the path that drops downhill with the hedge on your right. At the bottom turn RIGHT to cross a stile onto the track that heads under the railway then through houses on Dodds Lane to the main road in Craven Arms.

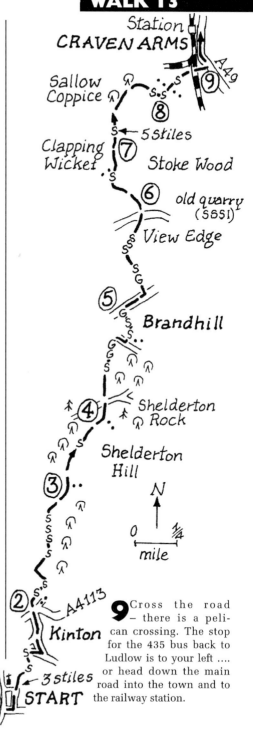

9 Cross the road – there is a pelican crossing. The stop for the 435 bus back to Ludlow is to your left .... or head down the main road into the town and to the railway station.

WIGMORE CIRCULAR

DESCRIPTION This 3 mile moderate walk explores the landscape surrounding the Norman stronghold of Wigmore castle where the Mortimer family ruled the borderlands for the best part of 500 years. The castle was eventually held by the Crown and then sold to the Harley family of Brampton Bryan who began to dismantle it during the English Civil War. Nearby stands the late 11thC church, funded by the Mortimers, and containing many monuments such as a rare piscina. The village includes a mix of old cottages and remnant orchards, some cherished and others neglected as well as new build on the east side of the high street. Refreshment is available from Mortimer Country Stores, run by the local community and specialising in local produce or the Castle Inn.

START & FINISH Castle Inn, Wigmore SO.416690.

DIRECTIONS There's a bus stop outside the Castle Inn but currently only market day buses call here, making bus access difficult. There is a limited amount of parking at the village hall just beyond the pub.

I From the entrance to the Castle Inn (formerly the Compasses), turn RIGHT and follow the road to the main road. Cross over and turn LEFT to walk towards Mortimer Country Stores but beforehand go RIGHT along a track which gives out to a path, often flowing as a stream after heavy rain. Go LEFT at a junction to climb up a corralled way, cross a stile and then onward over another to reach a lane. Go over the road, cross a stile and descend slightly LEFT down the hillside to a footbridge. *To the left, across the parkland, is Wigmore Hall, a 16thC half timbered house of distinction.*

2 Once across, climb up the shallow gully and then head very slightly RIGHT to pass by a cluster of trees to exit the field to the left of farm buildings onto the road. Take care here as the stile is at an awkward angle. Go RIGHT on the road and this soon begins to bend and descends towards Barnett Wood, known for its show of wild Lily of the Valley each Spring, but it is not your route. Beforehand, cross a stile on the right to enter a field. Head slightly RIGHT to skirt a corner of the wood and then aim for the top right corner. Climb a stile here and head slightly RIGHT across the field (locals walk the edge when in crop) to cross another stile by a gate. Bear slightly LEFT down the hillside into another gully where there's a stile in the thick hedge on the right. Climb this and go LEFT.

3 Cross the footbridge over the stream and head slightly RIGHT up the bank to eventually reach a stile by a rusty old gate. Cross the stile and follow the path through brambles to the road. Go LEFT to climb on this road for over half a mile. After passing the second smallholding on the right the road bends more and comes to another edge of Barnett wood. Cross a stile on the right by a gate here and head slightly RIGHT in the pasture, skirting the electric fencing and passing by an electricity pole. *There's a magnificent view of the castle keep from here showing what a formidable location Fitz Osbern and his successors chose.* Climb a stile and continue in a similar direction down the hill through rough ground skipping between nettles and thistles as you make your way to the bottom corner nearest to the castle.

4 Go through the gate and walk along the track to a kissing gate. Go through it and follow the fencing to another Kissing gate. Here, you can divert LEFT to visit the castle which overlooks Wigmore Lake (at one time it was a lake following glacial activity) and to the west are the Wigmore Rolls, wooded hills which make this landscape so distinctive. *The melancholy castle ruins belie the turbulent times witnessed in the medieval period when the Norman overlords sought to keep control of these precious lands. This was where the influential Mortimer family lived before spending more time at Ludlow Castle in the latter part of the medieval period. The compact quarter around the castle was at*

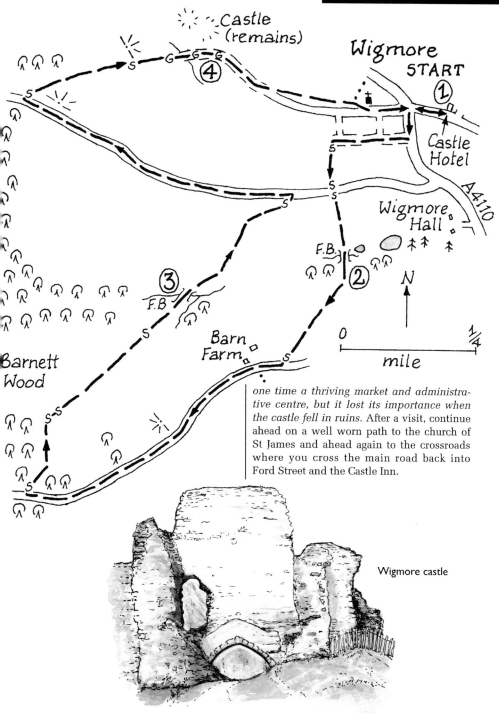

Castle (remains)

Wigmore
START
①

Castle Hotel

A4110

Wigmore Hall

④

F.B.

②

N

0 ————— ¼
mile

③
F.B.

Barn Farm

Barnett Wood

Wigmore castle

one time a thriving market and administrative centre, but it lost its importance when the castle fell in ruins. After a visit, continue ahead on a well worn path to the church of St James and ahead again to the crossroads where you cross the main road back into Ford Street and the Castle Inn.

YARPOLE CIRCULAR

DESCRIPTION A pleasant 5½ mile walk from the church in Yarpole with its detached timber bell tower and Gallery cafe (open weekday mornings), visit essential, before heading uphill for an airy tour round Bircher Common.
START & FINISH Yarpole Church SO 469648.
DIRECTIONS The walk starts at Yarpole Church, a ½ mile stroll from Bircher Corner on the 492 bus route between Ludlow, and Hereford (runs 2 hourly weekdays, fewer on Sundays). From Bircher Corner follow the sign to Yarpole, then take second road right in the village to the church. Limited on-road parking.

1 Leaving the church turn RIGHT up Green Lane past the Bell Inn. After Croft Crescent go RIGHT on path (waymark on left). Pass through a gate; walk across the field with a hedge on the right and proceed through a gate into woodland. The path narrows and then opens out at a house garden. Keep RIGHT crossing a wooden bridge to a garden gate and road. Take care as you turn LEFT for 20 yards, crossing to a footpath on RIGHT. Head straight across the field to climb a stile in the top left corner. Continue onward over a stile and then up the bank to a climb a stile top left, with house and barn to the right. Climb a stile at the end of this field then turn RIGHT onto a path at the top, joining a track past barns and houses.

2 At the third junction go LEFT past a stone block on your right. Follow this track as it curves left, ignoring the many grassy paths joining. This ends at a house where you go RIGHT on a grass path. Head uphill on a wide grass path opposite the next house. Emerge from scrub onto the well-cropped grass of Bircher Common turning LEFT. About 100 yards before the gate into conifer woodland, bear RIGHT uphill. Climb on the path round a copse of silver birch to the left.

Continue in the same direction when trees and scrub finish to the hill top with an excellent view of Titterstone Clee ahead.

3 Cross the common land towards a gate on the left where a path on the RIGHT heads towards the woodland. Follow this around the top of Oaker Coppice then down, always keeping the coppice edge to your right, ignoring all paths off the left. After a while you come to a seat and the view. From here aim half LEFT on the path heading diagonally downhill. This eventually bears RIGHT to join a stony track down to a telephone box and road.

4 Proceed along the road for 300 yards; where the road bends left turn RIGHT through a gate. With a hedge left, go down the field to stile onto the road. Cross carefully then go through a gate opposite to follow a waymarked path through fields. In the second field look out for a gate crossing the hedge RIGHT, then continue down over two stiles eventually heading to a gate in the field corner. The path turns left and heads out onto the road by houses. Go RIGHT, after a few yards RIGHT again into Green Lane and back to the church.

WALK 16

LUSTON TO ORLETON

DESCRIPTION An easy 4 mile walk between Luston and Orleton across mixed farmland on the Herefordshire Trail passing near to National Trust property, Berrington Hall. On the route it is possible to see Eye Manor and the remains of the Kington, Leominster to Stourport canal. It is easy to imagine what it would have been like walking down to market on these bridleways 200 years past. There is also refreshment at the Bakers Arms, Orleton.

START Balance Inn, Luston SO 486632.

FINISH Boot Inn, Orleton SO 491671.

DIRECTIONS Start at the Balance Inn, Luston which is on the 492 bus route between Ludlow and Leominster with a two hourly service on Mondays to Saturdays and a lesser Sunday service. There is limited on street parking at Orleton where it is also possible to catch the 492 bus from opposite the Boot Inn to enjoy this delightful linear walk.

I From the bus stop by the Balance Inn go LEFT along the pavement; opposite the Methodist Chapel turn LEFT through a barred gate. Go ahead to cross a stile and then head slightly LEFT across a large field. Go through a gap in the next field and ahead in a similar direction to a footbridge then ahead alongside a hedge on the left to cross a stile. Go over the railway tracks with care and cross a second stile. Continue ahead in a pasture to go through two gates and a farm track. Keep ahead again. Ignore a stile on the left, before going through a gate into the next field.

2 Go slightly RIGHT to look for a footbridge in the hedge seen ahead. To the left is Eye church and Eye manor, a Carolean period house once home to Jeremy Sandford, broadcaster and author of 'Cathy Come Home'. Once over the footbridge, turn LEFT and at the corner go RIGHT to follow the field edge to a track. On the left you'll catch a glimpse of the old canal in woodland on

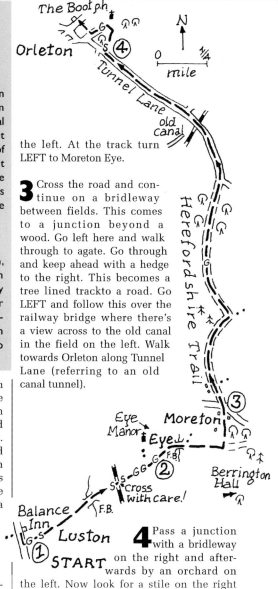

the left. At the track turn LEFT to Moreton Eye.

3 Cross the road and continue on a bridleway between fields. This comes to a junction beyond a wood. Go left here and walk through to a gate. Go through and keep ahead with a hedge to the right. This becomes a tree lined track to a road. Go LEFT and follow this over the railway bridge where there's a view across to the old canal in the field on the left. Walk towards Orleton along Tunnel Lane (referring to an old canal tunnel).

4 Pass a junction with a bridleway on the right and afterwards by an orchard on the left. Now look for a stile on the right opposite a sandstone wall and entrance. Go RIGHT over a stile and proceed ahead again and then slightly LEFT towards Orleton church. Enter the churchyard and walk to the left of the church where you turn left through a gate onto a lane. Look out for a narrow path on the right between gardens; this descends to the Boot Inn, Orleton.

31

WALK 17

PRESTEIGNE TO STAPLETON

DESCRIPTION A moderate 6 mile walk from the old county town of Radnorshire, Presteigne, alongside the fresh waters of the River Lugg to amazing gardens known as Bryan's Ground (*limited opening*). The walk then climbs through Coles Wood in Kinsham to an isolated cottage – Noisy Hall – before returning via Stapleton with its haunting ruins of a castle. There are no refreshments available, but Presteigne has a number of cafés and pubs; try the Gallery Café Bar at the Industrial Estate near the Recycling Centre.

START & FINISH Presteigne Bus Stops at the Recycling Centre SO 314642.

DIRECTIONS Start the walk from the Recycling Centre bus stops. Buses from Kington, Knighton and Leominster. There's car parking there and by the Police Station.

2 Go RIGHT along the road and you'll soon come to Bryan's Ground on the right. Described as a quintessentially idyllic English garden by one writer, this is not overstating the appeal of this superb 3 acre garden which has been in the making for 100 years. If you'd prefer to do a shorter walk (3 miles) you can always simply walk

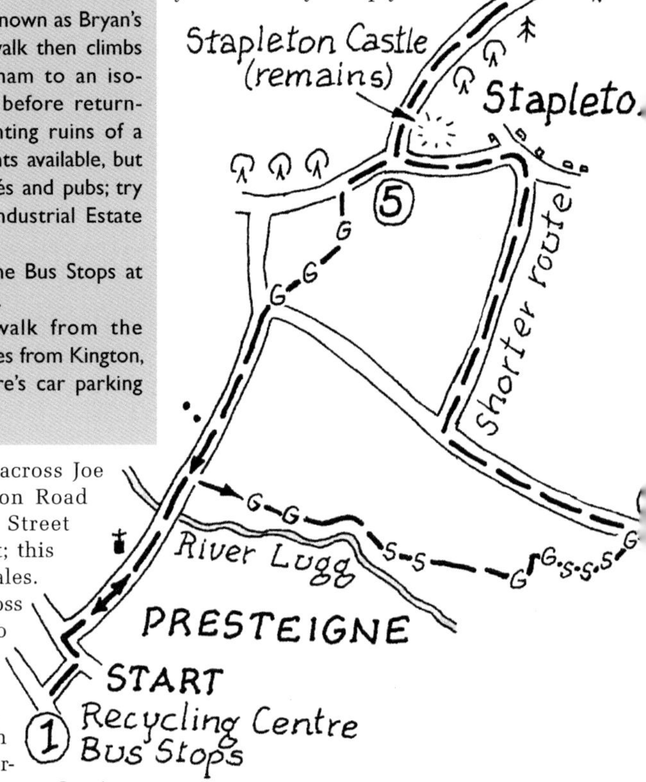

Stapleton Castle (remains)

Stapleton

Shorter route

| From the bus shelter go across Joe Deakins Road into Station Road and then LEFT into High Street and RIGHT into Broad Street; this part of town is firmly in Wales. Follow this out of town, across the Lugg Bridge back into England! Look for a footpath on the RIGHT along Brink Lane. This comes alongside the River Lugg then through a kissing gate and along a corralled path to another kissing gate. Continue to cross a stile and turn RIGHT on the lane (there's a dwelling to the right) and then LEFT over a stile by a barred gate. Keep ahead with a hedge on the left. At the field's end proceed through a gate and go LEFT on the road. Turn RIGHT at the next junction and just before the house, go LEFT through a small gate into a field and make your way RIGHT to follow the hedge to a stile. Cross it and proceed to cross another. Go over a drive and cross another stile. Head slightly left across the field to a gate leading onto a lane.

River Lugg

PRESTEIGNE

START

1 Recycling Centre Bus Stops

back along the road to a crossroads where a track is off to the left and a bridleway to the right. Go RIGHT up the bridleway and at the road turn LEFT to pass beneath the ruins of Stapleton Castle and then follow instruction 5.

3 If you are up for the full walk then continue ahead along the lane for almost a mile and at the junction turn LEFT. Walk up the track, go through a gate and turn LEFT. Ignore the next turn right. Keep ahead along a track which offers great views across a

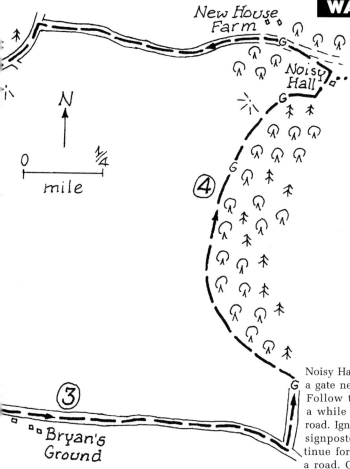

New House Farm

Noisy Hall

④

③

Bryan's Ground

N

0 ——— ¼ ——— mile

secluded valley beneath a canopy of trees. The track leads through Coles Wood to a gate and into a pasture.

4 Follow it up the valley to a gate and a made up forestry track. Keep ahead, ignore the first turn right and then take the second RIGHT and go first LEFT on a lesser track to rise up to another forestry track. Cross this and walk up a rougher green track towards the wood's edge. Just before, go left as indicated by a waymark on a tree and keep ahead on an indistinct through scrub, keeping a path ahead alongside the boundary to Noisy Hall cottage. *The name is unusual; it may be derived from the word noisette, meaning nut.* Go LEFT – there is a wooden waymark post here – up a lesser track above

Noisy Hall. You soon go through a gate near to New House farm. Follow this track ahead. After a while it becomes a metalled road. Ignore the track to the left signposted to houses and continue for around half a mile to a road. Go LEFT to descend to Stapleton. *There are great views from here across the Radnor Forest and the Whimble above New Radnor in Powys.*

5 The road comes to a junction where you turn RIGHT. Those on the shorter walk will also join at this junction and keep ahead. *Above stands the ruins of Stapleton Castle, built in medieval times but then turned into a more comfortable fortified house in later centuries. The remains are private; there's no access.* As the road bends to the right go LEFT along a path between and fence and hedge. Continue through a gate and head slightly right across a field to cross another. Make your way through a gate and turn RIGHT then LEFT at the junction to walk down the road back into Presteigne.

WALK 18

SHOBDON CIRCULAR

DESCRIPTION This 4 mile easy walk allows an exploration of the farming country beneath Shobdon Hill Wood. This part of Mortimer Country holds great potential for longer walks through to Lingen and on the Mortimer Trail; there are leaflets available from Leominster visitor information centre. The highlight is when you come upon the folly known as Shobdon Arches and the magnificent Roccoco style architecture to be found at Shobdon church.
START & FINISH Village Stores SO 398618.
DIRECTIONS The start of the walk is at Shobdon Village Stores on the B4362 where refreshment is available. The 493/6/7 bus from Leominster stops just 2 minutes away at the Grove. This operates on Mondays to Saturdays only. There is a limited amount of on-road parking in the village.

I From the village shop go RIGHT to walk along the pavement past the primary school. Just after, cross the road to walk up School Lane. The path runs alongside a dwelling at the top on the left to a stile. Cross this and walk ahead with a hedge to the left. Soon, go LEFT to cross a stile and then another soon afterwards. Continue along a hedge to the right to enter Shobdon golf course (care for there might be flying balls). Now proceed ahead with a hedge on the left but cross over to a corner where there's a white marker post. Continue ahead on this permissive path with a hedge to the right until you reach a stile. Cross it and go LEFT along the field's edge. On reaching a corner by the wood, go over a stile into a pasture and continue ahead. Cross a stile into rough ground and the path winds LEFT. Cross another stile and go RIGHT along the fence to a signpost. Head slightly LEFT to now climb a stile in a hedge. Proceed ahead to go through a bridle gate and Downwood Farm is across the field.

2 Head slightly LEFT in the pasture to cross a stile beneath a hedge. Now go slightly RIGHT across a field. Proceed through a gate and head slightly LEFT to a barred gate. Go through and cross the road to walk up the drive towards Belgate Farm. At the junction, go LEFT on a track which rises up and bends right. However, you keep LEFT here through a barred gate and up to a field.

3 Go RIGHT just beyond the line of hawthorns. Continue ahead with the hedge to your right. Proceed through a gate and ahead in the next field to go through another gate. Aim slightly RIGHT to the corner to cross a stile. Walk through the strip of woodland into a field and then cross a stile on the left into Shobdon Hill Wood. Turn RIGHT on the track and follow this to a gate leading into a forestry establishment. Go RIGHT to wood's edge to cross a stile to re-enter the field. Turn LEFT and continue ahead to reach a barred gate. Go through it onto a road and turn RIGHT to walk to a junction. Go LEFT and walk through the hamlet of Uphampton. The road bends and passes the entrance to Uphampton Farm on the left. Look for a signpost on the right as the road bends left. Follow a woodland track ahead through to parkland and turn LEFT to come to the Shobdon Arches. *The Arches are the remains of the old church which was replaced in the mid 18thC. These were saved from the original church built for the Norman overlord Oliver de Merlimond and exhibit some fine work which is now very weathered.*

4 Go RIGHT at the Arches to walk down an avenue of trees to a road junction. Keep ahead but on the left you'll see Shobdon Church which is a must to visit. *It was built in the 1750s by the Bateman family who at that time owned much of the land here. It involved Horace Walpole and the 'Taste Committee' and the interior was designed in the style of Strawberry Hill Gothic with soft*

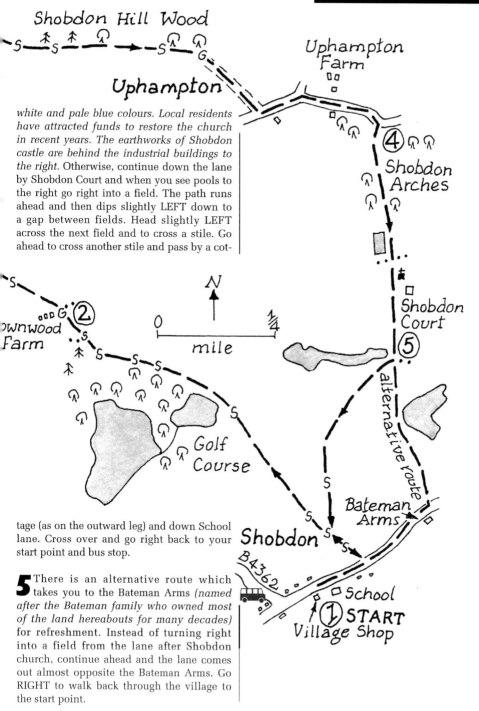

Shobdon Hill Wood

Uphampton

Uphampton Farm

white and pale blue colours. Local residents have attracted funds to restore the church in recent years. The earthworks of Shobdon castle are behind the industrial buildings to the right. Otherwise, continue down the lane by Shobdon Court and when you see pools to the right go right into a field. The path runs ahead and then dips slightly LEFT down to a gap between fields. Head slightly LEFT across the next field and to cross a stile. Go ahead to cross another stile and pass by a cot-

Shobdon Arches

Shobdon Court

N

0   ¼   mile

Ownwood Farm

Golf Course

Bateman Arms

alternative route

tage (as on the outward leg) and down School lane. Cross over and go right back to your start point and bus stop.

Shobdon

B4362

School

5 There is an alternative route which takes you to the Bateman Arms (named after the Bateman family who owned most of the land hereabouts for many decades) for refreshment. Instead of turning right into a field from the lane after Shobdon church, continue ahead and the lane comes out almost opposite the Bateman Arms. Go RIGHT to walk back through the village to the start point.

START
Village Shop

35

KINGSLAND TO MORTIMER'S CROSS

DESCRIPTION This 4½ mile easy walk includes a stretch of the Roman Road, Watling Street West and passes by the site of the bloody battle of Mortimer's Cross in the War of the Roses. It returns via the Lugg Valley to the pretty village of Kingsland where there are several half timbered and Georgian buildings and a church with a curious little chapel. There are several places to take refreshment on this walk, for example, the Garden Room tea rooms as well as the Angel and Corners inns at Kingsland. En route you'll pass near to the Mortimer's Cross Inn and the Buzzards holiday accommodation which includes an organic and biodynamic smallholding.

START & FINISH Corners Inn S0 444615.

DIRECTIONS The start of the walk is at the Corners Inn, Kingsland on the B4360. The 493-7 bus from Leominster stops here. This operates on Mondays to Saturdays. There is a limited amount of parking near Kingsland church.

I From the entrance to the Corners Inn turn RIGHT, cross the road junction, and walk ahead along the pavement until you see an entrance to a field between two bungalows on the left. Go LEFT here and then head slightly RIGHT across the field to the far right corner. However, the farmer asks that, when there's a crop growing, you use the permissive path alongside the right hand hedge to reach the same place. Cross a stile in the corner and go RIGHT to cross another. Now keep ahead to cross a third stile into an orchard. Head very slightly RIGHT through the orchard. Go over two stiles in succession to a grass verge by a main road.

2 Go RIGHT on the verge to a lane on the right. At this point, go over the main road and cross a stile by a drive leading to a house. Head slightly LEFT, cross a stile by a gate and then RIGHT over another stile.

Keep ahead with a fence to the right and conifers to the left; go through a gate into the next field where you continue ahead. Climb a stile to enter Mortimer Park – *the home of the Luctonians Rugby Club.* Walk ahead to pass to the right of the cricket pavilion then proceed through a gate. Continue ahead with a hedge to the right along a large field. Cross two stiles at a small coppice by a barn then keep ahead again across a pasture to a stile which leads onto Watling Street West. *This Roman Road linked Bravonium (Leintwardine) with Magnis (Kenchester) and this section is known as Hereford Lane.*

3 Go RIGHT to walk along this quiet lane for the best part of a mile. *Before you come to Lower Cross Farm the fields to the right are thought to have been the main site of the Battle of Mortimer's Cross in 1461, a bloody encounter by all accounts. It is said that the waters of the River Lugg ran red from the wounded and dead. There was also on that cold February morning a parhelion or 'sun dog', where three suns could be seen in the sky. The Yorkists took this as a good omen and they won the battle that day but not the war.* The lane meets the main road. Cross with care. Go over the stile in the metal fencing and head half LEFT across the field to cross a stile by barred gates. Those seeking refreshment should cross the road and go LEFT to the very friendly Mortimers Cross Inn. Otherwise, turn RIGHT to walk along the verge and over the bridge. Mortimer's Cross Water Mill is opposite, but is rarely open.

4 Go RIGHT over a stile and RIGHT again to join the riverbank which you follow at first. However, you soon leave it, up a slope, to go parallel to the river to another stile. Cross it and turn RIGHT to proceed along the field's edge to go past a wooden gate on your right into the next field and onward to cross a footbridge and bridle gate. Keep ahead in the next field to pass through a barred gate and follow the fence on the right to cross a stile. Continue ahead again for about 100 yards then go slightly LEFT to rise up the bank to a group of oak trees. At the top turn RIGHT and then proceed ahead through a

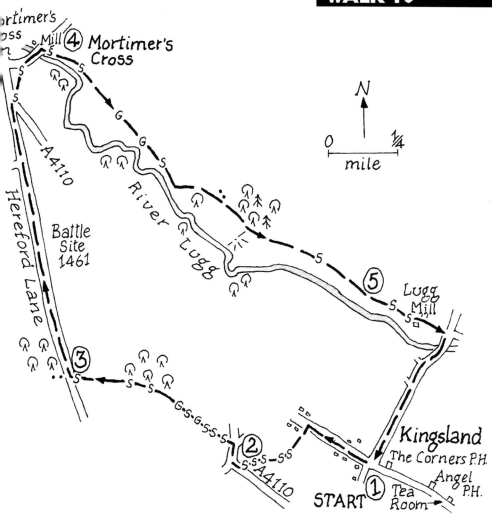

gap (where the stile has been removed) to the boundary of Tars Coppice. Follow the edge until a waymark post is reached (before the end of the wood) then head slightly RIGHT across the field to descend to the lower field boundary, aiming for the right hand end of a fence. Cross the stile next to a gate and continue near the fence on your right.

5 At the end of this section of the field turn LEFT, then almost at once RIGHT into a wood and emerge into a field to cross a stile.

Go ahead again through a small pasture to another (awkward) stile at Lugg Mill. Cross it and follow the path ahead by a building onto a drive and continue along this to a road. Turn RIGHT here to walk for half a mile into Kingsland. You reach a crossroads by the Corners Inn, where there's a bus stop. Kingsland has many half timbered houses and a fine church with its famous Volka Chapel, which to this day offers a service to commemorate those who fell at the Battle of Mortimer's Cross.

WALK 20

LEOMINSTER TO KIMBOLTON

DESCRIPTION A moderate 7 mile walk across gently undulating countryside from the historic market town of Leominster. This walk was inspired by a Leominster Apple Fair event, a great festival each year which includes several walks at this Walkers are Welcome town. The area is known for cider apple orchards found on the route to Kimbolton church, known to Wordsworth, and then near to Stockton Bury gardens where there's a café/restaurant. There's also an opportunity to call into the Stockton Cross public house at Stockton for a spot of refreshment.

START & FINISH Leominster Railway Station S0 502589.

DIRECTIONS Start the walk is Leominster railway station which has a regular daily train service from Ludlow; it takes eight minutes. Don't attempt to park at Leominster station. There's a car park on Broad Street 10 minutes walk away. There's also a two hourly bus 492 (less frequent on Sundays) from Ludlow to Leominster bus station (5-7 minutes walk).

I From Leominster railway station go ahead to the main road, turn RIGHT and at the corner by the White Lion public house, turn RIGHT on a path leading over the railway footbridge. The path (Herefordshire Trail) then bends left over a bridge. Once over, turn immediately RIGHT down steps and walk ahead alongside the River Lugg, through an underpass (which sometimes floods!). Keep ahead between the river and woodland planted by the Woodland Trust in 2000. At the end the path curves RIGHT to cross a stile and footbridge. Continue along the field edge and before reaching a stile onto the A44, go LEFT to cross a stile onto the pavement by the road.

2 Go LEFT along the road for 100 yards. Go LEFT through a gate and up a green track then up steps into woodland and then slightly LEFT up the bank to cross a track

and upward again to a stile. Cross it and keep ahead in the field to the corner where you go LEFT through a gate and then RIGHT over a stile. Go a few paces then cut slightly left across the field to a green strip on the other side leading down to a gap into the next field. Proceed ahead with a hedge to the left and make your way through a gateway and turn RIGHT, across a bridge and then LEFT to an old oak tree where you aim slightly left up the field to a wood. Continue to climb slightly LEFT to the next field. Keep ahead with a hedge to the left to cross a stile onto a road.

3 Go LEFT and then RIGHT to enter a wood. Continue ahead on a clear path to exit over a stile at a crossroads on tracks. There's a chicken rearing shed to the right. However, you go LEFT along a track between the wood and apple trees. This curves and passes to the left of a storage shed. Continue ahead to the end of the orchard where you cut RIGHT and within 100 yards, go LEFT through a gate. Keep ahead on a path that dips and then climbs on a track past two dwellings to a junction with a road. Cross over and go through a gate. Proceed across the field a similar direction towards a stile by a gate. Climb over but be careful as there's a drop down to the road.

4 Go RIGHT and then immediately LEFT to follow a quiet lane by orchards down to the Yolk Brook. Just beforehand, go RIGHT over a stile and walk ahead to go through a gate into an orchard. Continue ahead towards the stream on the left and at a hedge dip down to go through a gate into the next field. The path eases away from the stream up the bank and then slightly LEFT towards a brick cottage. Go through a gate, turn LEFT to drop down to a footbridge over a stream then continue ahead on a bridleway to a gate. Pass by Minnalls Farm to the main A4112 road

5 Cross the road and rise up the lane ahead. Opposite a house, go through a gate on the left into a field. Aim for the church and enter the churchyard through a gate. Exit onto a road, cross over a stile and walk ahead in the pasture. Cross a stile into the next field and head LEFT down the hillside to a point between two trees. Go over the footbridge spanning the infant Cogwell brook. Cross a stile into a field, go ahead at first with a hedge to the right until you reach a stile. Do not cross it. Cut LEFT to cross a stile in a fence. Head slightly RIGHT up a bank to cross a stile to the left of an oak. Go along the field's edge on the left and cross a stile and ahead to another by a gate. Head slightly RIGHT (of a bungalow) to exit over a stile by a gate onto a road. Go LEFT to the Stockton Cross Inn. *A few minutes walk along the road on the right leads to Stockton Bury Gardens, open to the public in the summer.*

6 At the junction, go LEFT and cross the main road to walk down a lane on the

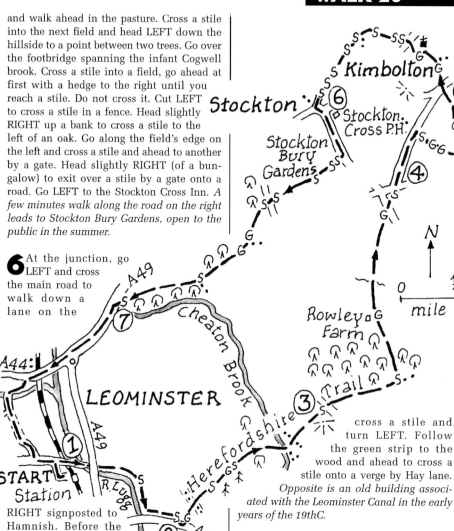

STOCKTON Kimbolton Stockton Cross P.H. Stockton Bury Gardens · Rowley Farm · Cheaton Brook · LEOMINSTER · Herefordshire Trail · A49 · A44 · START Station · R. Lugg · N · 0 ¼ mile

RIGHT signposted to Hamnish. Before the bridge go RIGHT over a rare step stile and another stile in succession. To the right are the grassy earthworks, all that remains of a deserted village. Go slightly LEFT to cross a footbridge. Head slightly RIGHT up the bank, cross a stile and keep ahead with the brook below. Leave the field over a stile by a gate and go over the road to cross another stile. Head slightly LEFT of the winding stream across a large field to the far corner. Go through two gates in succession and then ahead alongside the stream to a concrete bridge. Go over,

cross a stile and turn LEFT. Follow the green strip to the wood and ahead to cross a stile onto a verge by Hay lane. *Opposite is an old building associated with the Leominster Canal in the early years of the 19thC.*

7 Turn LEFT to walk alongside the A49 to a roundabout. Cross over with extreme care and continue ahead on the road towards Leominster. Go over the railway crossing and then look for a path on the left before a red brick building. This leads to an old iron bridge across the River Lugg (known as the Kenwater here) and up to Church Street. Go up steps to skirt the priory and keep ahead, across Pinsley Road to The Grange on the left. At the corner cut LEFT on a town path to a cul-de-sac and ahead to Etnam Street. Go LEFT to walk back to the railway station.

PRONUNCIATION

Welsh	English equivalent
c	always hard, as in **c**at
ch	as in the Scottish word lo**ch**
dd	as th in **th**en
f	as f in o**f**
ff	as ff in o**ff**
g	always hard as in **g**ot
ll	no real equivalent. It is like 'th' in then, but with an 'L' sound added to it, giving 'thlan' for the pronunciation of the Welsh 'Llan'.

In Welsh the accent usually falls on the last-but-one syllable of a word.

KEY TO THE MAPS

- ➡ Walk route and direction
- ▬ Metalled road
- - - - Unsurfaced road
- •••• Footpath/route adjoining walk route
- ∿ River/stream
- ⋏ ☘ Trees
- ▬ Railway
- **G** Gate
- **S** Stile
- **F.B.** Footbridge
- ⩊ Viewpoint
- ⓟ Parking

THE COUNTRYSIDE CODE

- Be safe – plan ahead and follow any signs
- Leave gates and property as you find them
- Protect plants and animals, and take your litter home
- Keep dogs under close control
- Consider other people

Open Access
Some routes cross areas of land where walkers have the legal right of access under The CRoW Act 2000 introduced in May 2005. Access can be subject to restrictions and closure for land management or safety reasons for up to 28 days a year. Details from www.naturalresourceswales.gov.uk or www.naturalengland.gov.uk. Please respect any notices.

Published by **Kittiwake Books Limited**
3 Glantwymyn Village Workshops, Glantwymyn, Machynlleth, Montgomeryshire SY20 8LY

© Text & map research: Les Lumsdon and Peta & Phil Sams 2014
© Maps & illustrations: Kittiwake-Books Ltd 2014
Drawings: Morag Perrott
Cover photos: Main: Ludlow & Titterstone Clee from Whitcliffe Common. *Inset:* Leintwardine Bridge. © David Perrott 2014

Care has been taken to be accurate. However neither the author nor the publisher can accept responsibility for any errors which may appear, or their consequences. If you are in any doubt about access, check before you proceed.

Printed byMixam UK.

ISBN: **978 1 908748 19 5**